HOLDING HEAVEN

a collection of poems

Elsa Mondou

Legacy Book Press LLC
Davenport, Iowa

DEDICATION

To Wesley and Beth, and to Phil, Christine, Mike, Julie, and Martin, and to all those whose being is incense to the soul.

TABLE OF CONTENTS

Holding Heaven

I do believe that
I am holding heaven.
A downy head,
Deep resting
On my shoulder,
Arms gently laying
Crisscross
Against my neck,
And the dear, quick
Cadence of breath
In sweet repose.

To cradle thus
And rock so soft.
A lullaby to hush
As lashes droop
And weight melds
To my form.

I will always remember
That peace
That love
Simply being one,
Together as one
As
Fundamental as the tide.

When you have loved
Like that
You will always
Love
Them.

Because they are
Part of your heart,
Part of your soul,
Part of your being.

And that is why
I know
That
I am holding
heaven.
When I caress you, dear babe,
You are
In my heart
Though maybe unaware.

And someday
That gift of
Being so cherished
Will be a blessing to you,
And tenderly in your arms
You
Will hold
Heaven
Too.

Hermes

Under the live oak they come,
first with wings upon their feet,
then the dutiful,
dedicated cadenced steps,
sprint at the finish.

And a contingent,
not gifted in flight,
but present in soul.
These are the spirit runners.
Those, tasked not with talent
but who deliver the message.

Of heart,
of iron,
of toil, sweat, longing,
and sheer will.

They run in mind
and drag the body after.
So every step in pain
is an act of courage.

Running not from great ability,
prowess, or gift,
but because it is a statement of fortitude.
Each step as if treading on fire.

And I watch…
Not knowing which is more admirable,
the incredible talent,
that unaware glides
past to finish
first and faultless
gifted and glorious
        or
the spirit runners,
whose every step
imprints perseverance
on the redolent earth.

Amid the din of laud and honor for the Hermes,
they pass on,
a beautiful, tortured passage.
And my eyes are wet
with tears of respect,
my throat dry…
as for the indigenous and buffalo,
migrating birds, and Monarch butterflies,
and golden beaded rain
that moves mountains into sea,
for a monument is passing by.

Providence

At times, life is like an arabesque over a waterfall,
a beautiful and daring dive
passing through kaleidoscope prisms
of light into free space…
all gold and red and glorious burnt umber.
Solace of rising mist and fresh burst
of clear, knife-edge air,
over the chasmed rock.

And mellow moments too,
the soft summer sun of a late August afternoon,
stroking the land with pastoral light,
and undulating shadow.
So welcome, the filtered light
through the piney wood,
caressing the face like a mother's kiss,
totally cherished.

At times it seems the blush of promise is forever ours.
To harvest as the stalks flower and ripen,
and savor as the glorious surge
of autumn color lights the hills.
So sharp and clear the carpet,
like many colored pebbles in the stream bed,
splashed as a painter might upon the canvas.
Bright, ethereal…such a precious, transient beauty.

And then it is winter…
the spike of cold, bright, piercing air,
diamond, crystaled snow, and glass ice.
The fine lace of frost spindling across the pane,
and the sun like spun gold
behind the cold, sharp peaks,
touching their slopes with the last rose rays
and promise of swift darkness.

It is a marvel in life to see much, yet understand little.
The light is everywhere and we at cusp,
catch glimpses as blue fire in the facets of a diamond.
As if one were on the wings of the wind, transported
through vast vistas over oceans fathoms deep,
yet can perceive only the glorious dazzle
of reflected light from surface waves,
with so much more beneath.

So much wonder,
complicated fractal riddles infinitesimal to galactic,
immense and infinite, so rich the diversity,
a masterpiece, a tapestry without a thread.

The light of the centuries is in the skies.
Millennia course through space to our vision.
Where are we then in this web of eternity?
The receiver and the giver of the light we have.
Like the magi bearing gifts
and following the star of promise,
we journey here to share our souls,
our being, and our truth.

We must so touch the world with gentle care…
so that we bestow a ripple on the pond's still water.
Insubstantial, transient, but spreading…
a perfect ringed distortion through the surface.
Wrinkling the image to a pentimento of the sky,
and fracturing the reflection with an impressionist's
flicker of the brush.
We are like a thread of the spider's web,
or the dew about to fall from the grass blade.
Each drop mirroring the cosmos.

All we can give is ourselves: love, delight, compassion,
…our soul which is light
that is the miracle we can bestow…
and forgiveness, love's best gift
for the forgiver and forgiven,
for we are one, completing the circle
of attempted perfection. We are mystery
and our life, the unconscious acceptance of the divine.

We would be the personification of joy and dance--
as light shimmering on the water
through the morning fog.
We are the fragrance of the myrtle in the dale,
sharing the perfume of its essence
without any purpose...but being.
All true beauty simply is.

So we must live with abandon and without fear,
and share our spirit as a banquet
for those around us.
It is the light we are gifted with,
and its glow must
shine through our lives.
Our destiny is to be
foam upon the wave,
dashing evanescent to the sand.

A pearl of great price this kingdom,
to be glimpsed, to be shared...
so real yet inexpressible
save in poetic memory
as untouchable as great clouds
billowing in the sky
and outlined with silvered light blown
surfing to the sun.

And when we die, shall we leave a trace
like mist upon the rocks of the waterfall,
prisming light and forming golden rainbows?

Yet, if we would keep our life safe,
we should surely lose its essence.
Life is a symphony and a dance upon the precipice.
There is a need to soar in fugue of flight
with no ownership for truth or love.

It must spill out in abundance as a great fountain,
rising like a Phoenix from the ashes.
We have a golden key that leads
beyond our definition of ourselves.
And if we ask, God will abide with us
and we shall be
the imperfect vessels
through which his light will shine.

A Secret Joy

If there is a benediction in life it occurs
when the heart sings,
when the soul laments or thrills an ode to joy.

It is when we are most vibrantly alive, aware,
vulnerable, quaking, expectant
like a hummingbird, beating its wings
in quick cadence before the flower--
so fast, beyond our ability to discern.

There is specialness in each of us,
a secret joy to be sensed,
a fragment of unconditional love
driven deep into our soul,
incense for our mind and essence of our being,
placed in our spirit when we were woven in the womb.

Nature bears the same secret promise.
Acorn becomes oak and there is the joy
of seed sown and grain reaped,
of renewal in the sweet loamy smell
of sod after warm rain,
of rivulet to river passing inexorably,
effortlessly on to the sea.

All is connected…
shoots from stump
pine from cone
life from death.

A sense of magnanimity is so close to pain.
Fulfillment so close to loss…
emotion pierces the soul
and we are made to see beyond looking,
coming to cusp, the precipice, the questioned destiny.

It is then that querying light shines out
as silent prayer from our eyes.
Indeed, we are an aberration, unique and distorted
as hand blown window glass…
waiting to stir the sunlight into flame.

But it is because of this…humility that we can make
whole the rent spirit of another--
that we can spiritually touch with grace
another's inner soul,
and soothe and balm that pain,
that secret fear we sense in fractured spirit.

Where does it come from—that spark of life in our soul,
the trigger point, the fire of our being?
It is not from us, but through us,
borne of love of the Creator.
We are the imperfect vessels though which
His light must shine.

Dear God, grant that we may oil the wood in our life.
Let us patiently craft a life of caring, and…
polish us with the wind and the sand of your Spirit,
so that we may be, someday…wholly yours.

Whither?

Diverging in the wood I turned
And looked to see a passerby,
My wish a wisp
In spirit's eye.

"Do you know the way?"
Quothe I,
"For path unsure,
Diverse is here."

I take my compass
From the sky,
But cannot
Know whither
Hence is good.

The horizon melts in field of trees,
Rich spires
Prick the clouds it seems.

I cannot see the place
I seek,
Though what I seek
Is far from me.

"Well stranger,"
Quothe the sage,
"I see,
You do not know
The way
Except the path."

And with a choice
So wide and free
It baffles first
And after laughs.

I cannot say
Which one to choose,
For either way
Is gain or lose.

This I do know
As I peruse
The path
Once chosen
Has its cost.

Fear not, however,
Gentle soul,
For every path
Its purpose spends.

And weaving threads,
And various light,
In dappled wood,
And wrinkled sand,
Provide an imprint
Be what might
The will for good,
Will ever stand.

A spirit humble
Knows not the way,
So pays attention to each step,
And graces every passing fern
With softest touch
Of sweet lament.

So steps do build a path upon,
And in the end a better way,
Than if the end were known before-
Without the search
And longing for.

Blue Mystery

Freely set sail
though never know
wind's measure--
how the shifts of sea
may twist and turn.

Destinations promised
currents pressure--
storms and tempests
rage leave ship
marooned.

So in what place
were we intended--
in our purpose
the one we
sought to seek?

Or were that paradise of land
in which we stranded,
the object of our heart's delight
to meet?

Wisdom would speak
to us of former,
Eden favoring the
latter hand.

Grace of God
or foment of disaster,
point of view
beyond a strip
of sand.

When in purpose,
doubt the measured
matter,
narrow focus
miss the eye of truth.

Only yours
through triumph and disaster,
perilous design
from treasured youth.

Think we that
we know the measure
of our bearing,
seeking sight
and fathoms deep to sea.

Humble now for we
are raindrops falling,
gathering
in beneficence to Thee.

Amaryllis

The ship is parting from the shore
and sails beyond in search of hope…
into the sun–through splitting waves,
the spray thrown high upon the prow
with glistening mist an aura round.

So vast, so silent is the sea
and we in the midst can't see the end,
so great is this infinity…
A touch, a brush of truth we grasp,
but for the rest it is all–
the rise and fall
and rise and fall
of endless waves undulating round.

But then there is a peace in this,
a rocking place for the soul,
to know that it is safe here to dream…
it is alright because there is no more pain
and no more anguish.

The ship is parting from the shore
to the hidden place in each of us.
Deep inside the soul, a sea inside a sea…
to the amaryllis in our hearts.
Red flowered velvet to the touch…
passion of our being and precious truth.

The amaryllis is our essence,
the harp that makes our spirit sing…
if only we could play its melody
and let deep joy shine forth.

Arrogance

A perverse year,
everything opposite of what
it should be.
Stupidity celebrated as insight,
and power invested in the inept.

Always prefer to be the last lemming.
But still most miss the crowd,
and traverse the cliff
with collective purpose.
That's instinct for you.

Born different,
but always desiring acceptance.
A paradox because
hallmark visions
rest in the unique soul.
Contemporary is confined.
Breakthroughs beyond grasp of hailed authority.

Hot like an oven,
people justify themselves.
Whatever their current view
of insight is--
blindness usually.

Shepherd

The shepherd was the best
he could be.
But no one knew it.
That is what made him so special.

Of course, the sheep were aware,
inasmuch as could be,
that their guardian
was a brave man
of loyalty and love.

There were other shepherds
who ran in danger.
Still others sold out,
and some who boasted
were Big Fish people.
The kind who caught
a minnow and
claimed a whale.

It was odd that his value was never noticed.
Perhaps people were too distracted
by the din of
wannabes or their own importance,
that they missed the real McCoy.

True treasure is not always perceived,
Even when it's obvious.
How else do we accept
miracles as ordinary?
Fail to celebrate a sunrise
or marvel as the sun
sets its curtain closed?

Blinded...
for the knowledge of that fruit
was for making Eden Hades.
A place of division
born of arrogance.

The shepherd was the best
he could be.
But no one knew it.
That is what made him so special.

He was who he was,
authentic to what mattered;
without ever
needing to
be known
to be so.
That is to say he had true freedom
and fulfillment--
because, after all,
both he, and we are on loan to this world.

Watershed

A warrior always has the heart of a lion,
even within the fleece of a lamb.

To be fierce,
there is no need to be strong,
just true.
And that's rare.

So what is the Litmus of life?
The cornucopia or courage,
the essence of the pearl of sand.

Watershed,
walking in the hurricane with a candle
to answer a far cry.
Valor palpably confronts fear.

Courage acts in vulnerability and knows misfortune.
On thin ice stepping out,
and claiming no loftiness
without conceit or artifice.

Seeing others as worth saving,
keeping word in derision,
and knowing no guile.

Of equal good in public and private,
unknown in the day,
with greatest laurels unsung,
though not unmarked by unconscious history,
indelibly imprinted.

Those who would claim to be
are mostly devoid,
for source lives apart from laud and honor.

As a force of nature,
like ocean currents, fault lines, tectonic plates,
shaping the geography of mind,
and the pageant of mankind;
we know indeed
where golden mettle's touch has been,
years hence.

The Path

I see the golden stair of raptured leaves
black printed with generous clay.
The path into the golden wood, the garden of
swinging birches and brilliant maple leaves.
So crisp the walk as twigs snap underfoot
my way is marked with slight impress
upon the rich yellow veined canopy beneath.

What trees along the farm field
stand as sentinels of frost.
To yield to wind and sing
the whispered delight of gentle breeze.
Crisp air like sweet cider
and lacing branches dappled light.
I would disappear into that splendored dawn.

Again, at night I chance to visit the same path
By harvest moon and light of snow;
now fall has passed to winter.
Sharp crunches underfoot and glittering shadows,
peace of night beckoning to stillness,
crystal cold and sharp, the good earth sleeps in frost.

And are our lives not so beautiful and strange?
Of many vistas seen and few paths chosen.
Of wonders yet unknown for what may be.
Of seasons kind and seasons frozen,
Of love besought and lost and born again.
Shall we not break the light
in prismed rainbows through our soul?

Intrepid

My soul in stillness waits for peace
in deep canyons echoing
in caves where moisture drips for centuries
and years are measured in centimeters of many hued
hanging rock.

In the still night a whisper wind
passes through the pines
and stars spiral overhead, shining ancient light.
Past is present here--
but future is unknown.

Yet it is not the future that we crave, but a direction
pain of purpose
and choices for the road.
We seek and trust that finding is our goal
when searching is.

So are we sunset and dawn,
Edgetones of spirit,
Wisps of painted cloud--
red, blue, purple
gilding edges of Earth
flaming briefly a beginning and an end.

We are unfinished carpentry,
but become complete by living
through suffering, despair, and joy
as the unfurled leaf, the cactus flower,
the flaming red of maple leaves
are beautiful because of their promise,
evanescence, and…fragility

So quiet this cathedral of woods--
shimmering light filters through balsam, fir, and birch
shafts through shadows
to highlight fern and moss.
Seemingly random, yet not so.
For there is more purpose than chance
on this good Earth.

We are meant to be transformers here--
Funnelers of pain,
changing that bitter fruit, injustice, or hurtful sentiment
into something kinder, softer, more merciful,
bestowing some gentle touch of caring
reaching to undo and heal…

But the energy of peace is not from us
but through us
the symphony of life is played
with imperfect instruments
made whole by the Creator.
A spiritual alchemy--
the solace is in the loon's cry, the waterfall,
the gentle cry of peepers in the spring.

Indeed, we could be prisms here
through which this light will pass and split
into rainbow iridescence—the promise of the ages...

Soul Search

The green place for the soul is touchstone of the spirit.
In suffering we go to an oasis of the mind,
a secret inner place of peace.

The soul travels to the familiar haven; passes beyond
care and distraction through timeless winds,
bestowing crisp coldness
like the savored sweet of autumn apples.

In the mind's eye appear the peaks of the ages,
rough granite in clouds, mists which hide but sooth
the naked rock—flame of maple
and butter yellow of birch,
the panoply of colored trees that quilt
the rolling play of hills and mountains.

In pain we remember the great grasping peaks
brushing the sky with majestic spires of sheer rock--
thousands of feet lined sharp and fine against the sky,
unreachable, untouchable, divine.

Sunset glows in the west
and stretches yellow and orange light
in swaths of cloud.
Majestic, complete, evanescent,
a silvered close to day.

The golden sky is mirrored with a great band
of sea blue peaks between sky and ice.
Slowly the sunset fades from gold orange to scarlet red
as the last rays blush the sky, and shadows lengthen.
Bleak winter winds blow snow across the frozen lake.
It is the beginning of darkness.
The soul yearns to follow the light,
to freely go as birds in fugue of flight.

Fractal landscapes,
infinity upon infinity the more we gaze.
A superficial glance masks infinitesimal handiwork.
Complexity is multiplied as we magnify our view,
our window to truth, our effort to see God.

From mountains to aspens to veins
in the quaking leaves--
ever-changing, pulsing, a transient perception.
The rich tapestry of dynamic change is life,
which we accept without knowing or understanding,
for life is the unconscious acceptance of the divine.

And man is spirit also.
Have you not seen the light in our eyes
leap forth in fire when we reach the heart
with care and touch our truer selves?
The shining of the spirit bespeaks our immortality.
Although distant, the inner fire of love is there
to be reached, felt, and shared.

Lord, if we could find a way around our lesser selves
to touch the spirit and the soul, see light of truth again,
past care and distraction to steward time here for you.

Oh Lord--
what would you have us do in this place?
How should we love you?
Only in humility may we see you Lord.
Only in the loss of ourselves in darkness
can we truly see your light.
Our despair makes your hope our promise
and your gift a saving grace for us.

We have the compass but not the key to open the door.
The light at tunnel's end masks boulders in the way.
Oh God, is it the path or the beacon that is important?
Indeed, the humblest things seem the most significant,
the small kindnesses, the lesser cruelties,
the tiny beat of insect wings that formulates a storm.
So unpredictably and secretly
the gift is given that we are unaware,
oblivious to the touch an angel
or the hairsbreadth difference marking life and death.

Veritas

At day's end when the sunset flames forth,
all adorned with gold, red, and purple hues
like a prism splitting light against the hills,
one asks—which light touched the spirit more?
The brilliant illumination of high noon
or the splendor of sintered light through clouds.

We are a kaleidoscope.
Many pieces and myriad patterns,
like dappled light playing through the canopy of leaves,
or wavering through water in undulating script
beneath the waves upon the sandy shore.

Oh God, you created us for your joy,
and inside instilled a splinter of your truth,
deep in our souls at the very heart of being.
A pearl of great value that, as a grain of sand,
is layered to rounded luster through our lives.

Each of us has a special vision,
a unique and separate strength,
but an imperfect soul that yearns for peace,
and an understanding of imperfection.
Diamonds and moon rocks, so rare and precious,
yet evanescent and insubstantial as mist or cloud,
or ocean spray with the gulls crying cadence
swirling high on the ocean's breath.

Oh God, as we run this race for you,
we would so wish to let the truth in our soul sing
with the perfect chords of a virtuoso,
spiraling with such beauty as mists the eyes.
We so wish to sprint with joy and embrace this world
with miraculous and healing touch.
So much do we wish to be whole and to make whole.

But the beauty of our life will never be perfection.
Our masterpiece is the pentimento, the artist's sketch,
the sweat and dedication to the truth and compassion
embedded in our spirits.

Since you gave us freedom
we are in equipoise.
There is no faith without fear,
no joy without sorrow,
and no love without deep pain.
And in the end—there is death to set the spirit free.

Why is there such anguish?
Is it because radiance is manifest in darkness,
and suffering and despair?
Is this what makes compassion shine from us
like the morning star?

In this life we can hope to touch others
with deep mercy, and chase impartial truth,
will all our hearts, souls, and minds--
like Magellan, to the ends of the Earth.

But our perception is not always truth.
It is what we see and understand of truth,
colored by desire or myopia of the mind--
set from fear or pretense.
But despite all, deep truth is recognized
because it resonates in the intellect
like echoes through chasms deep.
It is as a mountain,
genuine and irrefutable.

In the end we may never finish the race--
not by choice but by impediment or flaw.
Perhaps what is most important while life lasts
is the quality of our being.
The fragrance of our spirit rising fresh--
as the scent of wet earth and dew on the grass,
or the sweet perfume of the myrtle and velvet rose.

Sometimes we give by simply being.
And when we die, maybe we will be judged
by the quality of our love--
agape—the love of God, fileo—the love of befriending,
and the love of truth and faithfulness…
If only—if only with all the words in my heart,
I could make it so,
Semper Fi.

Angel

Come, oh angel of my heart
For your love touches all.
Light my spirit like a hearth
And shine within like stars of heaven.

Be light to my eyes
So to transform with tender alchemy
All pain in others that I see.
Make me a conduit of peace--
Of joy and love fulfilled in thee.

So much more to love than
A kiss, a smile, a tender longing.
It is a desire to make whole
And so to be whole…
Rising like the sweetness of Pachelbel's canon.

To heal a person, you must first love them
And so it is in loving dual healing comes,
And suffering melts away.
So it is that forgiveness is for the forgiver
And peace is in the letting go of pain.
That is why God came.

So then, what would I tell you before the night?
That I will love you always.
That if I could touch you with my soul,
Each day I would.
And that I am so very, very sorry for not being
Who I really am.

Come, oh angel of my heart.
Run and play with me.
Upon the shore where waves and breezes part.
Where seagulls wheel,
And sun fades fast
In scarlet flare
At the eves of the horizon.

Dance with me on ocean foam,
On the sun's rays
Like spun gold…
Mirroring the world
As dew on a web.

For I am like the dew on the grass,
Fresh and cool,
Yet evanescent as the wind.
Gone with a touch of the sun
And brush of breeze,
In the new dawn.

9/11

The explosion, the rubble,
the sound of shattered glass, and falling metal,
the tears in our soul blinding us,
closing the throat and shredding the heart with grief.
So many snuffed as a candle.
So much sorrow and pain to bear.
If only it could not be so.
Please God take it back.

So how do we who desire good dwell with this evil?
Surely, if war was desired it should not be granted
but we can't dance with the devil and not be changed.
We can't truthfully deny our fear
or our hearts split in two.
Yet we have destiny and choice before us--

To meet the cast glove with a dueler's bullet.
To skip reprisal in the name of compassion.
To discipline within the law.

How do we discern with wisdom and thwart evil?

So evanescent…
The insight is illuminated in glimpses--
Like the wavering shadow from branches
Tossed by the wind,
The rush of the wind in the pines
And the wisps of racing clouds before the storm.
So hard to grasp and hold,
It slips through our fingers as the fading rose and gold
Of sunset behind the mountains.

God, please help us discern truth and find courage.
To be wise and know that there is love
Even of imperfection.
That forgiveness is for the sake of victims—
So that evil can be transformed to good.

When we die, will we shine like the stars at night?
Will we break the darkness with our light?
God thirsts for all of us…
But it is now that we must shine so bright.
And share the gift of truthful sight.
To gift the world each day to bless
Each day we are to bless those around us.
Each day…

Newborn

When you were born
your childhood would be half
my lifetime.
All that could ever be imagined
was joy.

Warmth and togetherness
total acceptance
a microcosm
unto itself.

We would sit
and gently rock,
and I would sing
in low tones with you
draped over my shoulder
or cuddled at my breast.

The best moments
in my life were these
because they
were the purest
and in them
I loved most--
Not what you might become
but simply your being,
your soul.

Wellspring

I think I have always loved you
Dear child
As I see you nestled close to me.

So soft so tender to the touch
With perfect fingers
And dear toes
Like peas in a pod.

I knew you before you were born,
And you were so very much wanted,
A love child.

You look up and smile
Then sleepily
Turn your head and rest
With long lashes brushing rosy cheeks
And soft breathing like sweet summer rain.

Being loved like this is a gift,
One that lasts a lifetime.
It becomes part of you,
Being so loved.

This spirit
Interweaves in the fabric of your soul
A golden thread of joy
Like God's own mercy.

And because of tenderness and hope,
Nothing you touch
Will ever be the same.

My Child

Oh, how I would love thee, sweetest one.
There lying close to me with tender shared warmth.
All my dreams are with thee.
All that indelible love that will mark thy heart always.
Unquenchable, unconditional
A gift of safe harbor for thy soul forever.

What is it that makes us love so?
Is it that we remember our better selves,
And so to love with tenderest remembrance
Of holy wishing?

For you I pine with all my heart.
To caress, to kiss, to cherish always in my spirit.
I would so love thee that worlds could never end.
Least not the world I'm in.

So then where does the spirit dwell?
Between reality and another view.
A longing essence whose fire cannot quell,
The desire to share, serve, and burn in brilliant flame.

We are all angels here with choice of wings,
Whether to fly or forget their presence.
Golden light surrounds our heads
And shines in kindness through the eyes.
It is so with everyone who loves thus,
It is possible to see beyond,
This moment, this instant of distraction.

And God who thirsts and longs for us,
Surrounds our beings,
We unaware cannot perceive,
Yet He is there as silent soothing waters
Flowing round us
As imperceptible and subliminal as water to a fish,
As necessary as air for breath.
Ever-present, an unconscious incense for humility.

So then a life of mystic transit.
A journey, yet begun but of uncertain end.
For thee, dearest one, I yearn to guide, show the way.
Celebrating life, fearlessly spilling the heart like libation
Ever searching horizons yielding
To distant mirage and wavering light.
Spectrums of purpose and hopes for the soul.
Though it is for wisdom and peace we thirst like wine,
There is naught that could not be given
By so great a love.

Winter's Eve

Happy in the warmth of fire
And the glow of home.
Gentle lamplight,
And tender faces of the young.

A touch of frost and once again,
Crisp days and diamond nights,
Silent solace of the frozen northern lake.
Searing wind of memory
And crackling snow underfoot.

Deep within to be a child again,
And revel in a moment's bliss
Sledding on the hillside.
So sweet to laugh, and dance, and play
With no plan, no fear, and no regret.

Time stands still for me,
The instant caught in amber grasp
Spreading as soft ripples in the water,
Or the hawk's lazy swooping rings of flight,
Spiraling upward on the thermals.
Effortless eddies,
In cherished pause of mind.

Yet still nothing human is simple or effortless,
We are meant to strive for the good
We can perceive, but not yet realize.
So we reach and endeavor,
In measured steps of effort,
To the cadence of the dance of the universe,
And the rhythm we sense but cannot clearly hear.

We search and seek and so become.
We strive, sacrifice, yield, and surrender
As seasons turn,
As the tide flows,
As waves crash from aspiration to despair,
Movement, passion, and unease.

And yet nothing we ever do for love is lost.
For love of God or patient, stranger, neighbor,
Friend, child, parent, spouse.
Never truly lost...
Not one expression, touch, prayer, or embrace,
One dedicated sonnet, or discovery of truth or cure.

Winter's eve and the white cold drape will vanish,
To russet hues and splashing puddles.
The ice, like layered glass will wash to
Rivulets and gurgling streams,
That with tinkling laughter rush away.
Yet the perfection of the crystal snowflake,
Though evanescent, is not lost in this.
That kaleidoscope of beauty melts,
Caressing the earth with a wise, wet kiss,
Gently transforming it to spring.

Wedding

I kissed you once
And meant eternity.
That we would
Fall together
To embrace
A lifetime.

The best is yet to come
And we have come to be.
The aisle,
A path
To alter fate,
With promise.

Sweet melody
Where love is,
There we be.
Together
Dance
The fiddle medley
Fine.
And bittersweet
To twirl
In present mind.

Paint the stars
For me
My love.
Our wedding was
And memory
Has become.

Two to embrace
And
Walk
Together one
That path
Of sunlit gild on water set
That to horizon draws us close.

Incandescent,
We may not always be.
Passing…
As a strike of a match
At midnight.
But we shall always
Love,
Encompass twine
Much better than
Any other
Promise.

Be Still and Know

You were quiet there,
still in the magenta gown,
the one for our wedding.
So beautiful,
with laced flowers.

We filed by
and kissed you one more time,
the very last,
a tribute.
It was important
not to miss a chance,
for eternity.

Sudden, that news
when time stops.
When every rhythm,
all cadence gives pause,
cleaving the spirit,
so heartbeats melt.

Alone at night with fear,
closeted in ice come dreams,
pain of subconscious,
and deep questions of grief.
We chose to know death rather than God.
Why did we choose it?

Again, it is bright day.
Aged two years,
you are too young to know.
You laugh and run among
the cemetery stones,
as we lower her.

The earth is shoveled with dull, muffled sounds,
but over the heads of our gathering
I see you dance in the light.
Then you turn
and run to me,
your arms outstretched,
and my eyes mist,
And it seems…

That maybe the love we pass on
is all that really matters.
And perhaps by being empty,
we may see God again.
Because love abides forever,
in our memories,
and in our hearts.

Hidden

With caring face,
And firm embrace,
With warmth of strength,
And crinkled eyes,
You loved us in disguise.

In water's wake,
As cannonballs,
Like skipping stones,
Make splashing entrance,
Each one's turn,
You played with us.

With bait and hook,
The fish line in,
Drum, drum on sand,
In peerless moon,
We touch the silvered fish then free-
You told us give it liberty.

With grill and tongs,
With smoke and flame,
Or boiled noodle to your name,
You fed us out of love.

With discipline you taught and worked,
With chalk in hand,
And quiet grace,
Taught as a master would in place,
A labor that we did not see,
Brought wisdom out of misery.

And to your God,
Remained sublime,
In worship always,
Gave your time,
And to us all
You simply said,
To thank God
For our daily bread.

So kindly and so wise were thee,
And yet we did not come to see,
A present truth,
So plain before-
'Twas love that lit
Your heart's great store.

Seeing

I am about joy,
dancing on platitudes
and pirouetting on process.

An exuberance of life
cannot be hemmed.
The only control others have
is what we yield them.

Freedom is not a figment.
It is palpable and real.
The constrained life
is illusion.

Why would you abridge a sunset
for arbitrary caprice?
Or pursue a treadmill
to honor incompetent authority?

Such is to both desire and despise a mirage.
It is a hollow log
that bears no fruit.

Life is grace.
The creation is in green wood,
free flowering,
open to the sky.
The humble receiver
becomes wisdom's reservoir.

Query

If I were to love thee better,
How would it be?
Why when we love most,
We may show least?
Is it because we assume
Such a bastion
Of the heart,
Stands without telling?

Something so constant,
Like breath,
Is assumed
To be.
An understatement
Of the obvious?

Yet for those
Whose earthly tones
Desire living hues,
Whose strength of stay
Is like a field of rocks,
Proof be needed.

Is a life not enough
Proof of a love?
And of what substance
Are fetterments?

If we love,
But do not evoke love,
The love of being
Still remains.
A planetary force,
Like gravity.

Before Newton,
People did not know gravity,
But that did not
Change the fact
That it was
There.

So how can one know deep love?
Can a myopic man
Be the first to
See the mast
At harbor?

Was Beethoven's music
There for him to hear?
Deafening,
Yet present.

Do not presume to know
Only what your thought is.
The universe is
So much broader.

Infinite and
Infinitesimal.
Both
Directions.

Dark matter
And light.
Who knows
The which?

Majesty and
Brilliance,
Mist, sea spray
Rain
And
Glimmers
Of bright
Joy.

It all bespeaks
It seems
One word-
Wonder.

Seer

If I were to write a note
To press my future
Of wisdom gained,
In opportunity or loss,
What pleasant measure
My advice should offer,
Refraining solitude
Or bitter cost?

How to advise
A future holder's promise?
How to instruct,
Lest fame or fortune find?
How to enfold
The myriad of purpose,
How to embody
Mystery
In mind?

How can one know with
Heart so full to bursting,
All truths
Encompass
Threads beyond
Our touch?

How can one realize
Sweet truth
All transforming,
As bud in spring
To lushest
Fragrance lost?

We know the real,
Yet settle less for
Reasons,
We cannot fathom
Eden's way is spent.

And yet in moment's glimmer,
Light is fading.
In sunset rare
Our vision's
Sight is sent.

We would to God
For wisdom
And
For succor.

We would have always love
We dare to spend.

So let us dash
The fetters
Of our framework,
And seal our
Souls in light
That
Prisms
Bend.

Into the Light

When you love someone,
it is as if you offer your heart in a glass-
because you are sharing total truth,
the complete truth of your soul
and trusting, trusting, trusting...
that it will be understood and cherished.
Love is beautiful and painful,
and such a dangerous gift.
It is only made perfect in mercy and compassion.

When we first start to be, as children,
we love with unconditional joy,
without fear or boundaries, but endless possibility...
we can do this because we have the faith of innocence.
But the bravest love...
has knowledge and understanding--
and still in faith remains unconditional.

What is it that we love in one another?
Surely it is the spirit, the sensitivity of the soul...
truth, honesty, integrity, perseverance, wisdom,
courage, or perhaps an ability to see through
the heart and bestow peace.

Love, pain, and understanding are inextricably mixed.
In this world, depth of spirit comes through anguish.
It is the deep faults of the soul that move mountains...
and tear from our eyes the veil of distractions
so that we may see plainly.

Really, only God knows what love is.
Only he can touch the soul
and make it bloom as a rose,
or brush the heart to inspire love so deep,
that it is as precious and close as the dew on the grass.

If it is true that the kingdom of God is within us,
how are we meant to set it free and let it shine?
It would seem that we are as a candle
in a bell jar behind fragile glass.
So vulnerable to injury...but to the light,
the texture of the darkness does not matter.

So take courage tender heart,
for you were made for this and so much more...
deep anguish and vision
are the tonalities of light and shadow.
One cannot exist without the other.
Suffering is made precious
by its fragility, rarity, and uniqueness.
It is how we find faith as a gem
in the deep recesses of a mine.

Now we see the light as broken undulating shafts
shot through water and wave to the ocean bed.
It is distortion, but real and blessed.
Rippling through all creation,
through us, shining in our eyes...deep truth.

Essence

What endures?
Hope in darkness,
Mercy in adversity,
Courage for the dragon,
Will to persevere,
Love beyond self,
Trust in grace,
Kindness to bless tomorrow.

These are choices.
They transform,
As sticks build
A blaze
Upon coals.

But you have
To practice them.
Magic not of
Circumstances,
But of soul.

Life isn't about
Getting what you want.
It's about living,
And all that that means:
Pain,
Death,

Sorrow,
Suffering,
Fear,
Joy,
Creation,
Beginnings,
Dreams,
Adventure,
Fulfillment.

All on a knife point,
All of the time.
Kaleidoscopes of fractured hues,
Phoenix from
Ash to flame.

Pebbled patterns,
On the riverbed
Swirl with a current,
Unknown yet
Inexorably felt.

We must always choose,
Without knowing.
Cross the ice without
Sounding depth.
Cast the line
Fathoms deep.

It is the human condition
Not to know.
We chose it,
Long ago in the Garden.

And in this precarious
Universe,
We test the
Metal of
Who we truly are.

There is no courage
Without vulnerability,
No love without cost,
No loyalty without risk.

But because we are
Profoundly defined by such,
We must always choose.
To be is to choose,
To live is to choose,
To love is to choose best.

Within

What makes the soul to sing?
A bird, a breath, the waves, or call of gulls?
The baying hounds,
Or cacophony of geese?

What makes our spirit treble melody?
Were we strung as harps
Whose metal could not be silenced,
For we were made to resonate with timbered voice,
The message of our secret self?

What is it that rings within us,
That cannot be bound
But will express with even measured tones
And gentle harmony?

It is neither choice nor will
Can bend such expression.
It is through us like the pungent
Nectar of the lily
As inevitable as ripples of a stone's throw.

We cannot tell whence it comes
As from a wind that blows
From some way hence.
What fragrance it bears or kissing frost
to lay upon the blade.

These gifts we were born to sing
Within us as constant
As waves upon the sandy shore,
Crashing and tilling dunes to sea,
In endless cycling song.

As Near as Forever

Know that I am with you always.
As near
As the wind--
Rippling the grass blades,
Soft scent of gentle breeze,
And touch of sweet summer rain.

You are not alone;
Not in anguish
Nor pain,
For I am there too.
In the sunlight at daybreak,
First silver gold
Of dawn
And aura of the eve
Alpha and Omega.

If you really love
You will know me.
Boundless as the ocean
Depthless
Ethereal
Essence
Of all that is light
All that real love is.

Take courage, there is
So much more
Than you can
Possibly imagine,
Beyond the narrow
Confines of fear.
Even in the cadence of crickets,
The rhythm of
Waves and tide
And spinning mew of gulls
I am with you.

And so, the promise
Is yours to share.
Know that I am
Always with you
Even in suffering and grace.
And when you show
Real love
My light will encompass
Your soul.

Millennia ago
Wise men sought me.
And now you
Have become magi too,
Seekers
Finders
Sharers
With whom I abide.

Gift

To have one's meaning
measured in time's balance.
To call for worth
based on a transient moon.
To listen to whispered
pines in solace.
Knowing fortune's hand
may sever threads too soon.

In gossamer of forest
glade to wander.
While stars set gaze
upon horizon's path.
To tread upon the ocean foam and scatter
seashells and flotsam
in eclectic swathe.

To know by grace the pardon
quest would answer.
If but an affirmation
faith could see.
And how to reach the
density of matter.
Yet to become a man like thee and me.

If one were so to walk
with us unheeded.
Unrecognized by those
of maker's brand.
The irony of blindness
too conceited
to know celestial touch
by grace at hand.

To look upon the face
of divine sovereign
disguised in manger laid
and stable birth.
To take the humblest dwelling
rustic stated
and in divine indulgence
raise its worth.

For this the magi
harnessed camel,
and in night's promise
followed cosmic sign.
Searching as the
shepherds marveled glory.
Traipsing over
desert sands of time.

Though uncommon men
in understanding,
the gifts they bore
consecrated sight.
And to a king and prophet
priest they gathered
and worshipfully knelt
to treasured light.

And so in humble stall was given
the intersection
of all space and time.
The measure of all history divided.
The transcendence
of identity divine.

For finite time
we live and dwell in earthly capture.
Until we caravan
by star in homeward race.
And find ourselves
enchanted by faith's rapture
to behold in solace
once again His face.

Christmas Star

Star light, star bright
Let us see God's joy tonight.
Let us bless all those we see
Before we glimpse eternity.

The wise men followed such a star.
In trust they traveled very far,
And in the end your promise saw
A tender baby in the straw.

Summoned by the angelic host,
The shepherds came in holy fear
To wonder at God's humble post,
To tremble to see God so near.

A prophecy was by love fulfilled
In humility and dark concealed.
The pain of sin was washed away
By the miracle God wrought that day.

Let us be a beacon of your light
As your star was that Christmas night.
May we heal each other with your love
And trust your guidance from above.

Then Christmas will forever be
The path to peace for those who see,
A gift of spirit in manger laid,
The grace of faith for which we prayed.

Reverence

What is that sweet spark that saints have?
Of love and knowledge
On Earth and yet divine.

In wisdom to see all,
Yet like gold bear no tarnish.
To see evil yet
Transform it to the light

Where does this homing come from?
A reverential chord played deep within
With register upon registers of harmony
And octaves of depth.

How can we liberate compassion
Break through the seeping jealousies of time?
See through the glass of life so dimly,
Yet seek to speak and act the pure divine?

As lilies of the field breathe out our fragrance
And touch beyond all hope
The heart of good,
And close our eyes to whispered breeze in solace
To gently bear the hidden scent of heaven.

So shall we relinquish to reverence...
Since the very soul of worship is beyond ourselves,
It lies in the humility with which we seek
The sickle moon and fireflies
And surrender to awe.

Unknown

Don't you know…

There are some things one does for dreams,
     and others for unfathomable love.
And when the future is grey mist,
     it is fundamentals we are fond of.
It is those steps in blindness taken,
     that share our true intent.
In vagary of tide and tempest,
     wind's whispered conscience spent.

When we don't know where we're going,
     we may travel where we mean.
It is in fate uncertain
     that true character is seen.
In trepidation of dunes and desert,
     caravans come home to heart.
In our time of profoundest longing,
     find love's deepest gifts impart.

In mystery made perfect,
In uncertainty made rare,
In solemnity of forest,
In oblique despair in prayer…

It is when our soul feels smallest,
       that our spirit starts to sing.
It is when questions run deepest,
       that resonates our spring.

Season of Mystery

Though I cannot see or touch you,
my love ever remains.
And with it slowly growing,
peace in my life sustains.

Fragrant roses in the garden,
and rainbows in the sky;
the cadence of the dancing waves,
and mewing gulls fly by.

Still lightning laugher in the heavens,
painted sunset on the beach;
God's melody on Earth displayed
plays in my heart for each.

Each joy is in the 'morrow
and quiet blessings met;
the dappled light of forest,
the shadowed light offsets.

I know that Thou are with me,
no matter what I see.
I pray to God to touch me
so that I may be free.
And see the path
that led by Love
will bring ourselves to Thee.

Always

As each year passes by
We savor what's before.
We wish a happy birthday
And wish for many more.

If wisdom grew with years
T'would be no need of youth.
But time, a two-edged sword,
Divides between the truth.

With youth there is abandon,
Adventure without fears.
With age appreciation
Of happiness and tears.

We are in part a wonder,
A spinning loop in time,
And what we learn
And what we share
Are glimmers of divine.

So as buds to leaf acknowledge
The sun's new nascent heat,
We shall bring to fruition
Our balanced time complete.

In a circle we are woven
As loom and shears combine
To make wool for the fuller -
In fleeting stance of time.

So precious is the moment,
So spare seems yet the day,
We are lucky beyond measure,
Yet fail to feel that way.

In gratitude is glory,
In appreciation joy.
In grace to see the mystery,
Discern our hope employ.

As sunset burns the heavens,
As waves crash coral beach,
The start and end of lifetimes
Is timed as meant for each.

We would never know our meaning,
If time would never end.
We would never know
We loved so much
Unless we lost a friend.

In losses and in gaining,
The meaning matters much.
It isn't while we have them
To crave their loving touch.

If love and loss are linked
So they are sometimes all the same.
For to have them and to lose them,
They in our hearts remain.

Spirit of the Maple

I am a tree with my toes in the soil
and my branches soaring upward to the sky.
My leaves lift to the light
and the sun gives their verdant green pure energy.
My roots rest on the strength of the rock
and I stand like a statement forever in one place.

Though still, I am silently aware.
I see the world parade by my feet.
The squirrels scratch and scramble up my trunk,
and the birds flit about my branches,
pronouncing their delight in song.

The crisp days of fall come,
and I drink deep of the bittersweet coolness.
Green fades and my leaves flame red,
a color always present but never seen through green.
My leaves whisper in the wind and fall at my feet,
rustling at the softest tread of passersby.

Soon it is winter, and my limbs are coated
with glittering snow and ice.
And though I seem dead,
I sparkle as a diamond in the sun.
My spirit is silent, but I am here
for those with the gentle gift to see.

Snow Spring

Filtered grace thy fingers trace
And weave across the pane
The diamond-lustered paneled frost
Spun gossamer again

And sparkling shafts of gilded light
Through dappled forest glade
The eddying snow its crystals shake
From boughs with soft snow laid

The tender bush is gilt with ice
And blossoms ever frost
As if with laden buds in bloom
Snow flowered branch embossed

The purity of winter cold
As we drink deep its breath
Remembering in its vapored mist
Fond home and hearth our breadth

Of the cold nights and glittering days
And sunsets blazing bright
All hemmed in gold the rolling hills
Red hues reflected light

I would thee love with my whole heart
Whose beauty my heart sings
Of glorious truth and happiness
And cherished love it brings

Yet if we have but eyes to see
Humility of art
What everlasting joy is wrought
In every humble heart

Glade

Softness of wood
and glow of pine,
sun's brushed needles
sparkle and shine.

Chatter of brook
and chortle of stream,
solace, bliss,
reflected sheen.

Crisp hum of insect,
taut hoot of owl,
whispers the stillness,
be with us now.

Rings in the water,
steps in the sand,
breeze in our soul,
life in our hand.

Known in a moment,
lost and yet won,
whistles the spirit,
wisdom will come.

How can we find you,
whole spirit divine,
transforming of water,
life intertwined?

Present in quiet,
humble of heart,
love facing outward,
blessing impart.

With Quiet Courage

Inside of every person is a precious light
shining sweetly through the eyes.
It is the soul God loves
and would have us cherish in everyone.
And in every life there is a sign--
a moment, a gesture, serendipity,
a spiritual coincidence beyond hope and chance,
a time when God makes it possible
to continue beyond our strength.

Life is not about receiving our heart's desire
but about letting the light within us shine--
in blessing and through storms,
each day to touch eternity.

Today is special.
It is not just a 24-hour span
but an extraordinary gift.
When the sun rises, it is not just morning,
but the start of a new century, a new millennium,
the rest of eternity.

And we are not just breathing.
We are inspiring the sweet breath of plants,
mist of new rain, and fragrance of flowers.
What is around us is not just sun, sky, trees, and land.
It is a miracle in infinity and the infinitesimal.

Larger than we can imagine--
Light years through the galaxies,
yet also beyond the resolution of our understanding,
in subatomic space.

This is not just light we see
but all rainbow colors merged white–
images of ancient light and present reality combined,
a curious and wonderful world.

When we leave this Earth,
it is not death,
but a gateway to eternity.
We leave behind fragments of our soul's delight,
the blessings of our spirit
embedded in the hearts we touched.

For that is how we come to see God,
with quiet courage
over a lifetime.

Sunset

When painted sun strikes errant cloud
And wisps of pink about me shroud
The golden light upon the bay,
The sea and sky in endless play

To sit and contemplate the moon
Reflected image in the stars
The splintered glass of sunlit day
Reveals in night its bright display

And springtime's bud upon the limb
Lifts each branch skyward like a hymn
To burst its breath in fullest bloom
With fragrance sweet and lush perfume

And wonder of it all to be
A crystal soul divine are we,
To seek and spin, and kindle light
To cherish each with brilliance bright.

What truth may be for us to find?
Unique perspectives of the mind,
Or better yet, our spirit strives
To see all men through God's eyes.

For the Lost and the Living

As I look out at the horizons of our lives
It is like time travel
Wind sweeping over golden issues of waves
Cliffs rising from silhouette against a bronzed sky
Clouds lifted up in swirls and spirals
Of evanescent mist
Without boundary
Yet perfectly sharp from afar
But when entered blurred and mystical

What is the ache in my heart
That will not declare joy
In the deep breath of pine
Or thrill with the lament of the gulls at the shore
Or the ebb, flow, and roar of breakers meeting land

We are sun and moon and stars
All of the things we see and touch, care for and adore
We are compassion and beauty, hope and despair
We are the seekers for our destiny here

Do the stars sing beauty as a harp sweeps its chords?
Does the fall of each raindrop matter?
Does each dragonfly and dancing moth
Spin the universe?

All of us weave a cloth we cannot see
A gossamer carpet of inconsequential acts
A passing glance of kindness that costs nothing
But means everything.
Like myriad water droplets against the backlit light
Which makes a rainbow promise at the end of a storm.
Iridescent beauty yet made of light
And water of immaterial substance.

What we recognize as important is not so often so.
The kindness is in the little things a touch, a word,
A moment spared to really see.

It is so much better to understand rather than to judge
To love goodness into existence
For it is there always as a seed in the earth
We were made to give love more than to receive it
Out of an abundance of hope and belief
That light is in us all.
As innate as the uplift of wings in flight
Of the eagle soaring on the heat eddies
And thermals of the sandstone canyon.
We are the living water that quenches the need
Of the spirit to share love regardless of its reception
And to share our light regardless of its recognition.

A mountain in the mist rises solitary and loftily into the
rarity of the atmosphere. It is there whether recognized
or not and so are we. All life is golden and precious. All
life is possibility and a miracle of transformation. The

acorn into the majestic oak and back to Earth again. It has always been so.

But it is the love we bear that makes the difference that marks us. It is how much we care that holds us like the edge of a knife. Equipoise between good and evil like a great game of chess — we struggle to let our light shine.

But we do not write the book of our lives in solitary. We are given choices although the scenes of the drama are presented by fate. So we must know that the sun shines but does not worry about whether it is seen or not. All true beauty, all true good simply is. It is not subject to any judgment but its own veracity. What is genuine is true. The beauty and the intricacy of the kingdom are within us.

The leaves of the quaking aspen, the haunting cry of the mourning dove, the rumbled bass of a cat's purr, and the chime of crystal voices caroling, so much to hear and feel and cherish, so rich the expressions of creation.

We are light and joy and peace if we so choose, regardless of how others see or misinterpret us. It does not matter as long as we have a sense of what we truly are. We are the sunrise and the sunset, the joy of the scent of fresh mown hay and the delicate sonorance of wind in the willows. The laughter and freedom of the brook and the mystery of foam on the ocean or light from the stars that breaks into rainbow hues through the prism. We are richness beyond measure and love beyond all telling.

We are blessing and immeasurable sorrow, suffering that makes possible empathy and understanding. Love and pain inextricably mixed, and desire and hope made precious by despair. It is for the lost and the living to know this and it is not an instantaneous knowledge but grows over a lifetime. Every triumph is possible because of an experience of defeat that made it necessarily so. We are a tapestry of such richness and intricacy that it is an impenetrable design for the thread of its composite. We are the music of the universe and the dance of the spheres.

There is belief and desire, hope and despair in all of us. Like facets of a diamond, so hard and brilliant, complex and diversified, with fire so precious yet apparent only because of the light shed upon it. We are the raindrops of the storm, small, insubstantial yet in aggregate making a rivulet, stream, river, and changing the level of the ocean. We are important in proportion to the measure that we realize our belonging to each other and to this Earth and universe.

Our purpose is to pass our light, our love, and our belief on...all accomplishments are beliefs initially and all have their season and cycle. Dew to frost, green leaf to scarlet red and mellow gold of fall, innocence to knowledge, and passion to courage. The swirls of the hurricane on the skirts of the Atlantic, humility and acceptance. There is no knowledge without humility, no true leadership without some measure of consensus, no joy without suffering, and no understanding without effort. The light is all around us, but we are blind not by design but by choice. It is there in all of us, in all things living, in the earth, the petals of the daisy, the fragrance of lilies, the light of compassion. We know what true good is, we all know it...it is when the message and the messenger are one.

ABOUT THE AUTHOR

Elsa Mondou, like many, is a seeker, and these poems that are offered herein are simply that, an offering which was requested to be shared.

Before he died, Elsa's father had very much desired that these poems be published, and he was right; they are meant for everyone, to give light to the loved and the lost.

Made in the USA
Middletown, DE
05 July 2021